Boll Weevils

Jonathan Kravetz

The Rosen Publishing Group's
PowerKids Press™
New York

For Annie, who taught me to love gross bugs.

Published in 2006 by The Rosen Publishing Group, Inc.
29 East 21st Street, New York, NY 10010

First Edition

Editor: Jennifer Way
Book Design: Ginny Chu

Photo Credits: Cover, p. 17 © Alton N. Sparks, Jr., The University of Georgia/insectimages.org; p. 4 courtesy of insectimages.org; p. 5 © Academy of Natural Sciences of Philadelphia/Corbis; pp. 6, 21 Auburn University Libraries, Ralph Brown Draughon Library, Department of Official Collections & University Archives; pp. 9 (right), 14 © George D. Lepp/Corbis pp. 10, 13 Clemson University — USDA/insectimages.org, (inset) © Richard Hamilton Smith/Corbis; p. 14 (inset) Ronald Smith, Auburn University/insectimages.org.

Library of Congress Cataloging-in-Publication Data

Kravetz, Jonathan.
Boll weevils / Jonathan Kravetz.— 1st ed.
    p. cm. — (Gross bugs)
Includes bibliographical references (p.   ) and index.
ISBN 1-4042-3041-6 (library binding)
1. Boll weevil—Juvenile literature. I. Title. II. Series.

QL596.C9K73 2006
595.76'8—dc22

                                  2004021240

Manufactured in the United States of America

CONTENTS

Destroying Cotton Fields

Tarnished Plant Bug

Southern Green Stinkbug

Other insects attack cotton, including the southern green stinkbug, the grasshopper, and the tarnished plant bug. The boll weevil is cotton's most harmful pest.

Grasshopper

The biggest problem cotton farmers face is an insect that grows no longer than an eyelash. The insect is called a boll weevil, and it feeds on the seed pod, or boll, of the cotton plant. Female boll weevils also lay their eggs in the cotton boll or in the square of the cotton plant. When the egg hatches, the young, or **larvae**, eat the inside of the boll. This is where weevils cause the most harm to the cotton plant.

Boll weevils did their worst harm in the United States about 80 years ago. In 1921, U.S. farmers lost about one out of every three **bales** of cotton they produced.

Cotton Square

Small Boll

Flower

Leaves

Large Boll

The picture above shows the parts of the cotton plant. Boll weevils attack the cotton's squares and bolls. The square ripens into a flower and then into a boll. As the boll grows, it opens, and the cotton fibers grow out from it. This is the fluffy cotton that farmers pick. Although people do not eat cotton, it is considered a fruit.

The boll weevil migrates to find food. Boll weevils usually only fly short distances, but they can migrate nearly 200 miles (322 km) when helped along by the wind. In the above picture, this boll weevil has its two sets of wings spread as it would if it were flying.

Coming to America

Boll weevils **migrated** to the United States from Mexico, where they lived off cotton and wild plants. In the United States, boll weevils feed mainly on cotton because it is so plentiful. By 1920, they had spread across all the cotton-growing states, which include Texas, Mississippi, Virginia, the Carolinas, Georgia, Florida, California, and Arizona. They covered 600,000 square miles (1.6 million sq km) in fewer than 30 years! The boll weevil's spread across the South caused many cotton farmers to go out of business because of the harm they caused to crops.

Scientists **classify** boll weevils (*Anthonomus grandis*) in the Curculionidae, or weevil, **family**. With more than 40,000 **species** of weevils, it is the biggest family in the Coleoptera, or beetle, order.

Is It a Boll Weevil?

Boll weevils, like all insects, have a head, a **thorax**, and an **abdomen**. They also have a long snout, or nose, a hairy back, and clublike front legs. Boll weevils use their snouts for eating and for boring holes in which to lay eggs. Boll weevils have a pair of **mandibles** at the ends of their snouts, which they use for chewing and for making holes.

Adult boll weevils are reddish brown when they are young, but they quickly turn brownish gray. The body of an adult is covered with small, light-colored hairs. The hairs are thicker near the center of the weevil's thorax. This makes them look like they have a stripe down their backs. This stripe helps farmers tell them apart from other tiny insects.

The young boll weevil on the left is pushing its snout into a cotton boll in order to feed on it. Boll weevils have a double-toothed spur, or bump, on the side of each front leg. This can be seen in the picture on the right. The spur is one of the easiest ways to tell boll weevils apart from other types of weevils.

Spur

This boll weevil has made a feeding puncture, or hole, in the cotton plant so that its snout can get at the insides of the cotton plant and eat it. *Inset*: When cotton is ready to be picked, the downy fibers burst out of the boll. These fibers are picked and cleaned and can then be woven into cotton ... into clothes.

The worst harm the boll weevil causes to cotton plants occurs after the larva hatches inside the square or boll. The larva eats the fibers used to make cotton and the seeds that the plant makes. Adult boll weevils feed on the bolls, squares, and leaves of the cotton plant. Their snouts make holes, called feeding punctures, in the plant. When weevils attack crops, it is said that the crop is **infested**.

When cotton squares are infested with weevils, they turn yellow and fall off the plant. Bolls remain on the plant, but the larvae eat all the seeds and fibers inside.

A boll weevil monument stands in the city of Enterprise, Alabama. It was built in 1919 to represent the changes that were required after the boll weevil had destroyed so many cotton crops in the area.

Like many insects, boll weevils undergo changes before becoming adults. This process is called **metamorphosis**. The first change occurs when the egg hatches inside the boll or square. This happens three to five days after the egg is laid. The larva that hatches from the egg is white with a light brown head.

The larva lives and feeds inside the cotton boll or square. As it grows the larva casts off its skin three times.

After 7 to 14 days, the larva covers itself in a hard shell and becomes inactive. This marks the beginning of the **pupal** stage. This stage lasts between three and five days. Inside the pupa, the larva grows wings. When it comes out of the pupa, it is an adult boll weevil.

These boll weevil larvae are in little danger of being eaten by other animals. This is because the larvae are guarded by the cotton squares or bolls in which they are growing. Boll weevils have almost no natural predators, or enemies.

This boll weevil has recently come out of its pupa. Its reddish brown color will soon darken to the adult boll weevil's gray color. This takes about one day. *Inset*: Boll weevils that have just come out of their pupa sometimes rest in cotton flowers while their skin dries and hardens.

When the boll weevil is ready to come out of its pupa, it chews its way out of the square or boll using its mandibles. When reddish adult boll weevils first appear, their skin is not completely hard. Young boll weevils often rest in open flowers, where they can feed on **pollen** while their skin hardens. This takes about 24 hours. Once its skin is completely hardened, the boll weevil takes on its normal brownish gray color.

Boll weevils can grow from egg, to larva, to pupa, and to adult in fewer than 20 days. Female boll weevils can begin laying eggs three to five days after they become an adult. This means that several **generations** can be born in one cotton-growing season. Cotton is usually grown from May through the end of the summer.

Adulthood

The boll weevil lives for 44 to 55 days. About halfway through its life, at around 20 days, the weevil is an adult and can mate. Mating is joining together to make babies.

Their short life is an advantage to the species. Because there are so few days between when a boll weevil is an egg and when it becomes an adult, many generations can be born in a year.

Adult boll weevils grow and mate during the cotton-growing season. Luckily for farmers many boll weevils die over the winter. However, the adults can also sleep through the winter in a special state called **diapause**.

This boll weevil has the hardened brownish gray skin of a grown adult. Adult boll weevils can mate three to five days after reaching adulthood. The number of generations that can be produced in a cotton-growing season depends on the weather.

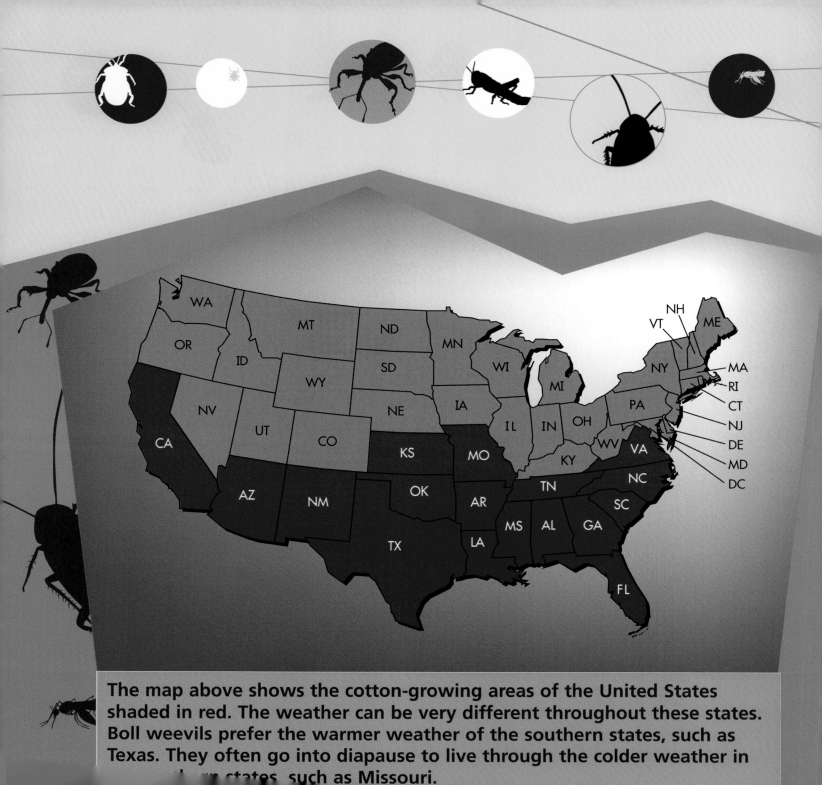

The map above shows the cotton-growing areas of the United States shaded in red. The weather can be very different throughout these states. Boll weevils prefer the warmer weather of the southern states, such as Texas. They often go into diapause to live through the colder weather in ~~~~~~~ states, such as Missouri.

Diapause

Although the boll weevil is mainly a hot weather insect and lives mostly in southern states, it can live through cold weather by entering diapause. Boll weevils enter diapause when the days begin getting shorter at the end of the summer. They prepare by feeding more. This helps them store up fat. Once it gets colder, boll weevils will find a warm place to sleep, such as in grass clippings.

Most boll weevils that enter diapause are killed by the cold weather. Those that live start to come out of diapause in early May. They come out of diapause throughout the cotton-growing season. The weevils that come out of diapause later have a better chance of living through weather changes early in the season. These weather changes can affect their food supply, the cotton plant.

Mating and Laying Eggs

In the spring adult boll weevils fly around cotton fields and feed for three to seven days. The weevils then mate. Male boll weevils produce **pheromones** that draw females to them. This pheromone can draw females from as far away as 500 feet (152 m). After mating, females bore into squares or bolls and lay eggs. They can lay about 12 eggs per day over 12 days. A single female boll weevil lays about 150 eggs during her lifetime. This means that in just five generations, one female boll weevil and her young can create more than one billion offspring!

Many female boll weevils will mate before entering diapause. This means that all they need to begin laying eggs the following spring is a supply of newly formed cotton squares.

These are boll weevil eggs. To lay eggs, female boll weevils make a feeding puncture in the square or boll. After she has fed, the female will lay a single egg in the hole and seal it with a sticky, gluelike matter. Females lay one egg in each boll or square. Other females may lay eggs in the same boll or square in which another female has already laid an egg.

How Boll Weevils Affect People

Farmers have tried many ways to guard their crops from boll weevils. One of the first things farmers tried, in 1899, was planting cotton crops early. They hoped the cotton plants could grow before the weevils could begin mating. This helped a little. Farmers also used **pesticides** to attack the young weevils, but it is very hard to kill boll weevil eggs and larvae this way.

In 1978, the U.S. government began a boll weevil **eradication** plan. First farmers spray cotton fields with pesticides. Then the farmers set traps. If the traps catch a certain number of weevils, the farmers know they need to spray again. By using this process, it is hoped that the boll weevil population could be greatly reduced in the United States within the next few years.

GLOSSARY

abdomen (AB-duh-min) The large, rear part of an insect's body.

bales (BAYLZ) Big packages of cotton used for sale.

classify (KLA-seh-fy) Arrange in groups.

diapause (DY-uh-pahz) A period when all growth is stopped.

eradication (ee-ra-duh-KAY-shun) Having gotten rid of something.

family (FAM-lee) The scientific name for a large group of plants or animals that are alike in some ways.

generations (jeh-nuh-RAY-shunz) Groups of beings born and living at the same time.

infested (in-FEST-ed) Spread over an area in a troublesome manner.

larvae (LAR-vee) Insects in the early life stage, in which they have a wormlike form.

mandibles (MAN-dih-bulz) The paired jaws of an insect that generally move side to side.

metamorphosis (meh-tuh-MOR-fuh-sis) A complete change in form.

migrated (MY-grayt-ed) Moved from one place to another.

pesticides (PES-tih-sydz) Poisons used to kill pests.

pheromones (FER-uh-mohnz) Chemicals produced by an animal that allow it to send a message to another of the same kind of animal.

pollen (PAH-lin) A powder made by the male parts of flowers.

pupal (PYOO-pahl) Having to do with the second stage of life for an insect, in which it changes from a larva to an adult.

species (SPEE-sheez) A single kind of living thing. All people are one species.

thorax (THOR-aks) The middle part of the body of an insect.

INDEX

A
abdomen, 8
Anthonomus grandis, 7

C
Coleoptera, 7
cotton boll, 4, 11–12,
    15, 20
Curculionidae, 7

D
diapause, 16, 19–20

E
eradication plan, 22

F
feeding punctures, 11

L
larvae, 4, 11–12, 15,
    22

M
mating, 16, 20
metamorphosis, 12
migration, 7

P
pesticides, 22
pheromones, 20
pupa, 12, 15

T
thorax, 8

Web Sites
Due to the changing nature of Internet links, PowerKids Press has developed an online list of Web sites related to the subject of this book. This site is updated regularly. Please use this link to access the list:
www.powerkidslinks.com/gbugs/weevils/